The Moral Vision of the Letter to the Hebrews

Greg Forster

Rector of Northenden, Manchester

GROVE BOOKS LIMITED
RIDLEY HALL RD CAMBRIDGE CB3 9HU

Contents

Acknowledgments

Once again, I am grateful to colleagues in the Grove Ethics group for support and encouragement as I have prepared this contribution to a series of studies on the ethical slant of the New Testament writings. Despite some delays and glitches in cyberspace they have made helpful comments, to which I have reacted, though not always in the way they expected. I am grateful for access to the John Rylands University Library in Manchester, without which this study would not have been as comprehensive as it is. I hope that I have treated the writers whom I have summarized in chapter two fairly, or at least piloted readers to where they can find the fuller version. My own reactions to the letter are in chapters 3, 4 and 5.

The **Cover Illustration** is by Peter Ashton

First Impression July 2005
ISSN 1470-854X
ISBN 1 85174 596 3

Introduction

1

In the Introduction to most commentaries on Hebrews you will find no section about its ethics.

In the index of most books on New Testament ethics you will be lucky to find half a dozen references to Hebrews. Look them up; many are dismissive. That says more about our perception of ethics than about Hebrews! It is a deeply moral book, revealing a vision of an ethical community, and offering intense motivation for moral conduct.

Hebrews is a deeply moral book, offering intense motivation for moral conduct

Hebrews is an enigma. No author identifies himself; neither destination nor origin are indicated. Its date can only be inferred internally — which presumes that we know the circumstances alluded to. Even the genre is uncertain, though the author does indicate his view. Perhaps this uncertainty is because he uses material honed in dialogue and sermon. Only at the end come the greetings characteristic of a letter.

Those final greetings (13.22) contain the author's characterization of the piece — a 'brief word of encouragement — *paraklesis*.' The readers need that encouragement because they are flagging in their *Christian* faith, pressured by growing threats of persecution and tempted to revert to the safer *religio licita* (permitted religion, under Roman law) of Judaism rather than stepping out of its safe camp to stand alongside God's true, new covenant people. Much of that 'encouragement' is an exploration of the truths about Jesus' person and work, which make their faith distinctive. This *paraklesis* includes a character-forming appeal to model their lives on Jesus, and other heroes of faith, and to live up to the community values which they had previously espoused. So the stirring theology of Hebrews is not an abstract exercise in dogmatics but is intended as an inspiration to perseverance (*hypomone* — a key New Testament virtue) in the face of moral, spiritual and real physical threats. Moral instruction and rebuke is inter-stratified within the theology of chapters

The stirring theology of Hebrews is not an abstract exercise in dogmatics but is intended as an inspiration to perserverance

1–10, as well as outcropping plainly in chapters 11–13. So we may accept that Hebrews arrived like a letter, but its writer perhaps imagined arguing it out in synagogue as he dictated it.

Their temptation was to revert to the safety of Judaism

I say synagogue advisedly, since his use of material and manner of presentation presuppose a familiarity with Jewish methods and an interest in Jewish concerns on the part of his hearers. Their temptation is not to opt back into *paganism*, but to revert to a *Judaism* in which they had been at home. If not ethnic Jews they were converts well versed in Judaism before acknowledging Jesus as Messiah. They were members of the church, but members inclined to meet among their own Christian Jewish circle more than with the wider church, who kept their lines open with their old compatriots. Their renewed interest in Judaism is not a desire to make all Christians conform to Jewish cultural markers. They are not like the 'men from James' of Galatians 2. Rather Judaism offers a means of safety in the face of persecution, and possibly a gateway into a profitable economic network. Our writer can refer critically to 'dead works' (9.14) and in more secure circumstances his readers would have agreed with that description of Jewish observances.

What were those circumstances? I find myself persuaded by John Robinson (*Redating,* pp 200ff) who sees the recipients of the letter as Christian Jews who are distancing themselves from the wider church in Rome as Nero's persecution (64–67AD) grows. The former trials of 10.32ff, when they had accepted the loss of property, are the disturbances which led to Jews being expelled from Rome in Claudius' reign. Jerusalem, with its sacrificial system, still stands—though later writers, Jewish and Christian, use an 'ethnographic present' to describe rituals which ceased when the Temple was overrun in 70CE, our writer's argument hinges on their passing nature; if they had already ceased it would clinch his argument to say so!

Robinson's theme is the date of NT books, but he permits himself to debate the authorship of Hebrews, and favours Barnabas, whom Tertullian (early third century AD) named without fear of contradiction when quoting our letter in a challenge to the Roman church—Barnabas wrote to Jewish Christians in the Roman Church, where Hebrews was quoted by Clement (*c* 95AD). If Robinson is right, it has interesting ethical implications (as he hints) since Barnabas—the 'Son of Paraklesis'—was well placed to write about generosity and sacrifice of property, and had a name for bridge-building. No argument can hang on this possibility; Origen was on safer ground when he simply concluded 'God knows!' (Eusebius, 6.25.13).

Whoever wrote it, the letter is an exercise in practical ethics, an example of how the Christian virtue of *koinonia*, sharing, is maintained in fraught conditions. It reveals a vision of the church that is not a mystical entity or theological concept, but a functional moral community which works by mutual support and encouragement, shaped by the achievements of its Founder. That it is not the normal view

The letter is an exercise in practical ethics, an example of how the Christian virtue of koinonia is maintained in fraught conditions

of Hebrews. Because its Christology is so inspiring, and because it deals in a unique way with the relationship between old and new covenants, there is a tendency to major on those features. A book on the *ethics* of Hebrews is perhaps pre-programmed to draw such different conclusions, but they are valid conclusions. As I suggest later, different writers' approaches to ethics shape their appreciation of the ethical value of any biblical book.

If Hebrews is a strongly ethical book, what does it say about our view of ethics if we fail to recognize that?

That brings me to a further point. If Hebrews is a strongly ethical book, what does it say about *our* twenty-first century view of ethics if we fail to recognize that? How does its two edged sword cut between the joints and marrow of *our* understandings of morality? In a society which sets high value on *individual* moral choices and responsibility what do we need to learn about shaping the moral *communities* which will shape us? How did our writer do this?

Finally where was it written? The author sends greetings from 'those from Italy.' This makes most sense if he is not in Italy but mutual acquaintances from that region are with him. Little in the ethical field depends on this.

2

What the Ethicists Say

As in previous contributions to this series, I will summarize the way various New Testament ethicists treat the letter, and set their comments in context since that tells us something about ethics today as well as about Hebrews!

John Murray: Principles of Conduct

This work gives an illuminating contrast to more recent studies. Though Murray only refers to Hebrews seven times in 269 pages, these references highlight a strand in the thinking of our author different from those discussed below, but significant nonetheless. Murray was professor at Westminster Theological Seminary in the 1950s, and might be described as old school Evangelical. He treats the Bible as a whole, and cites Hebrews to demonstrate that awe before God as judge is not just an Old Testament idea (p 234) (10.27, 31).

God's *holiness* should be central to our understanding of him and so his wrath rests with reason on sin. To fear him is an incentive to perseverance in faith and obedience (4.1). Both Old and New Testaments expect holiness from God's people, since God is himself holy (p 198) (12.14). It is a matter of spirituality within a covenant relationship to God, interwoven with obedience to the commands of God. It sets God's people apart morally from the world around. Hebrews insists that this holiness be maintained with perseverance; we cannot presume on past experience of grace (p 199, citing 3.14, 6.11, 12, and Col 1.22f).

Murray uses our author's encouragment in the face of temptation to answer 16th–20th century questions about lapses in morals and faith

Murray uses our author's encouragement in the face of temptation to relapse into Judaism to answer 16th–20th century questions about lapses in morals and faith, and the assurance of salvation.

J T Sanders: Ethics in the New Testament (pp 101-110)

Sanders sees Hebrews as an alternating pattern of theology and *paraenesis* (encouragment and advice) . 'The crowning point of the theological thought lies in the paraenetic portions.' He laments, 'unfortunately for our interest here...the *paraenesis* has precious little to say about one's ethical dealings with one's fellow men or with one's world, but deals rather almost exclusively with the strictly religious ethical concern that the congregation "hold fast" to its confession.' For the writer 'sin' is disbelief (3.12) while 'love and good works' (6.10; 10.24) are a category within 'keeping the faith.'

Sanders reckons that our author goes furthest among New Testament writers in transforming a futurist salvation ('Will you now restore the kingdom to Israel?') into a spatial heavenly hope ('you have come...to the heavenly Jerusalem, 12.22), but even he cannot dispense entirely with eschatology. In 10.25 the imperative of fellowship is motivated by Christ's imminent coming. Sanders is scathing about such use of eschatology, and suggests that this is not our author's primary intention, but that here and in chapter 13 the 'old' motives are too deeply ingrained in his own and his church's thinking to be omitted. In that chapter each example of moral conduct is a practical outworking of the main theme—keep the faith! But he relies on an inherited store of teaching, which he and his readers already know is right and which comes with its own equally inherited justifications. (So, in 13.4, marital fidelity is supported by fear of judgment, not the main theme of communal support and faith-keeping). Chapter 13 is not a loose appendage; it forms a logical conclusion to the homily—here are primary but largely random examples of how keeping the faith will work out in practice. It does not represent, however, a full programme for Christian living.

On that basis Sanders asserts 'It is not possible to derive any further ethical guidance from chapter 13.' Since he sees Hebrews as one of the latest items in the New Testament he concludes in pessimistic tones. In this reiteration of virtues the author finds himself (with the later 'Pauline' corpus) merely equating Christian ethics with good citizenship. (Earlier Sanders identifies *paraenesis* of this kind as a feature of Hellenistic Jewish homilies, and links it with Jewish and Stoic teaching on good citizenship). 'With this approach one no longer needs Christianity to propose an ethic of "the good."' In any case, Hebrews does not provide a lead for defining 'the good.' 'Christian ethics is now altogether awash. It lacks direction, motivation, even a *raison d'être*.'

'Christian ethics is now altogether awash. It lacks direction, motivation, even a raison d'être'

Earlier, in general discussion of 'the latest' NT writings, Sanders claims that the 'love commandment' is absent from Hebrews except as a 'dim memory' in 10.24 and 6.10. While *philadelphia* (brotherly-love) is enjoined, *agape* is merely correlated with good works; active, not emotional love is in focus. He does also acknowledge that our author encourages an imitation of Christ—but leaders from an earlier Christian generation are also held up for imitation.

Sanders claims that the 'love commandment' is absent from Hebrews except as a 'dim memor in 10.24 and 6.10

Sanders wrote in West Coast America in the late 1960s, early 1970s. Bourgeois was bad, radical good, divine imperatives suspect, and 'love' (as an emotion, more than as active care, it would seem!) was the key to morality. No wonder he was pessimistic!

From the same period comes Leslie Houlden's *Ethics and the New Testament*. His reference to Hebrews is minimal: it does not feature in his survey of 'The Writers' of the NT; the verb 'love' is absent; with other NT writings it shows an understanding of human weaknesses, but there is intolerance or perhaps despair over apostasy (p 99). He notes (p 72) a shift from love as *the* overarching Christian principle in early NT material to a situation where it is merely one of several Christian virtues in Hebrews and 'later' writings. '[Love] has lost the brilliance with which it stands out in the (early) books…'

Wolfgang Schrage: The Ethics of the New Testament

If one had no text of Hebrews, but only the comments of Schrage and Sanders to judge it by, one might ask if there were *two* letters of that name. Their views seem so different. Schrage notes the way moral encouragement is interleaved with high theology in Hebrews, but (p 9) even the Christological 'Hymns' (for example Phil 2.5ff) elsewhere in the NT are included only for their moral implications.

He sees the letter as an exhortation for the pilgrim people of God, for whom the eschatological hope is central

He sees the letter as an exhortation (*paraklesis*, 13.22) for the pilgrim people of God, for whom the eschatological hope is central (p 323). This hope (along with the idea that the son of God, the Great High Priest, understands and sympathizes with them) undergirds that encouragement. And God's people *are* pilgrims; the ethos our writer is propounding is one of mutual support, hospitality, encouragement and partnership for God's people who are distinct from the world (p 321, p 327). There is no vision of this world transformed; rather the hope of attaining the abiding city to which they travel. 'Though the epistle…is dominated by a spatial dualism of this world and the heavenly world, it breathes eschatological hope.' Judgment is a motive for this ethos, but a greater theme is this promise of good things to come. Since rewards (and retribution) are mentioned firmly our author is in danger of promoting a religion of works, despite his recognition of the prevenience of grace (12.28 'Since we are in receipt of a kingdom which cannot be shaken, let us have, or accept, *grace through which* let us offer our service worthily to God,' my translation).

Schrage notes how our author uses examples (and warnings) from the Old Testament to drive home his encouragement. Notable is chapter 11, but in 3.7ff the Exodus generation are a warning against apostasy, while Jesus himself is example as well as Saviour (especially 13.13—compare 1 Peter 2.21). The Old Testament and its law is seen as an earthly *and passing* good (10.1). Its moral and cultic laws are held together, but are seen as ineffective (not threatening), achieving only ritual purity, not a clear conscience; dead works are purged by Christ's sacrifice alone.

Schrage sees the influence of a 'popular philosophical ethics'…'looking to regulate middle class Christian life' in Hebrews. There is a dualism, paralleled in popular Platonism and in the Alexandrian Jewish writer Philo, in which this world is less real than a transcendent one. But the visible world *is* good, created by God's word, even if it will yield to one which 'cannot be shaken.' Our writer sees this view foreshadowed in the Old Testament as his heroes look forward to what is 'invisible, but to come' (11.25–27) The practical application is fortitude in the face of suffering, not the embrace of asceticism.

The practical application is fortitude in the face of suffering, not the embrace of asceticism

Though his phrase 'middle class Christian life' might sound dismissive, Schrage points out that it was *not* necessarily a conventional or widely accepted way of life in its day. There is a need for these Christians to 'stir one another up' to 'love and good works.'

Schrage has some helpful discussion of 'love and good works' (10.24, compare 6.10) 'The distinction between love and good works is not made clear.' Significantly love is mentioned first, especially if 'good works' is used in a Jewish sense to mean works of mercy. (Strobel [NTD 9, p 198] suggests that Hebrews follows a Jewish distinction, distinguishing between (works of) love, and good works inspired by moral choice rather than emotion. It differs from that tradition in not subordinating the former to the latter). Indeed, 'the epistle loudly proclaims love of one's neighbour as its primary goal.'

I find this affirmation, so different from Sanders' and Houlden's, somewhat surprising, since *'agape'* is rare in the letter and it is not neighbours (understood as fellow human beings, in the modern liturgical sense) but Christian comrades who receive *'philadelphia'* (13.1. In 6.10 'the saints' receive the service *agape* inspires).

Schrage discusses 6.10 suggesting (with 'many scholars') that some kind of financial support is in view, perhaps even the 'Collection' which played such a part in the early church (for example Rom 15.25, 31). (If so, then Hebrews is the first Christian example of the tendency by which the cardinal virtue of a faith comes to be seen in terms of financial 'charity' — love in Christianity, *tsedakah* [righteousness] in Judaism).

Schrage recognizes the centrality of suffering in the letter — not self-chosen asceticism but persecution, to be borne with fortitude in company with all God's people. In the context of a threatened church the weak are to be strengthened and peace sought with all (12.13f). The group to whom the letter is specially addressed should not stand aside (10.25). Indeed, Hebrews is an ethic of the people (or household, 10.21) of God.

So, finally, Schrage identifies the setting in which the author refuses to countenance a second repentance for apostates. Socially it would undermine the stable (middle class?) community. Theologically it would negate the unique effects of Christ's sacrifice. Yet his words are a warning rather than personal condemnation (10.39).

Richard B Hays: The Moral Vision of the New Testament

Hays' approach to New Testament ethics is different from that of his predecessors. It is one I find most helpful. He is looking not for a set of standards, nor principles from which to deduce conduct, but for the moral vision which inspired the New Testament communities in their Christian living. The NT is not (p 193) a dogmatic system (in ethics or theology), but a series of reflections on a common narrative — from creation through the call of the chosen people to Christ and his church, inspired by the Holy Spirit as a sign of God's redemption of the world. One can see the influence of the late twentieth century concept of theology as story and also a reaction against an earlier theology of love.

Hays finds three key lenses by which the NT vision of Christian behaviour can be brought into focus

Hays finds three key lenses through which light can be shone on the NT vision of Christian behaviour, or by which it can be brought into focus. These he finds by looking for features which are major themes in all the NT texts, which are not contradicted or rejected in any NT text, and are central to the moral argument in all of them. Thus 'freedom from law' is *not* one of the keys to the NT's moral vision, because in Matthew, James and the Pastorals it appears to be contradicted, despite its significance for other writers. Likewise the 'love command' is not central to Mark—12.28–34 is isolated; discipleship is cross-taking, not love. Nor is it central to Hebrews, where references to love are only scattered; only once is it an ideal (10.23–25). The recurrent ethical imperative is patient endurance, and while our author is not indifferent to love, the paucity of references to love is striking; the phrase 'love and good works' is a give-away—for him (as in Revelation) it is simply 'good behaviour.' Further, where Hebrews does focus on love it is to remind us that love calls for repentance, discipline and sacrifice; a transformation, not bland inclusivity (12.5–13, compare Luke 14.25-35). Love's meaning is found in Christ's cross (p 201).

However, if we use Hays' three 'lenses' which are central for understanding the NT's vision of the moral life, Hebrews immediately springs into clear focus, near the centre of the picture. One of those lenses is the cross; the other two are the community, and new creation. By 'the cross' he means that Christian discipleship is an imitation of Jesus, and the readiness of all the community (not just those already oppressed or poor) to suffer together. He cites (p 197) Ephesians 5, where the well placed husband not the socially weaker wife is called to Christ-like self-giving. He might have cited the way in which in Hebrews a secure group is called to come outside the camp to identify with Christ's wider, vulnerable community.

Hays invites us to see how the formation and maintenance of a new cohesive community is central to NT thinking. He points to the way Christians are called (Rom 12.1) to present their bodies (plural) as a (singular) sacrifice, and how images of the body, a building, a city and Israel itself are focal in NT thinking. He might have drawn attention to how our author urges his readers not to isolate themselves (10.25) from the new community (6.4–6), and features *philadelphia*.

His third 'lens,' the new creation, is the belief that the best is yet to be; what Christians experience now through the community is a foretaste of what is to be. For Hebrews this takes on a different dimension from most of the New Testament; the future hope of 'the day drawing near' (10.25) is overlaid with a Hellenistic view of a heavenly fatherland beyond the present passing world (11.16).

Hays concedes that these lenses are not moral principles in themselves, but tools for understanding and interpreting both the principles and the details of the NT's moral teaching. He also recognizes that they derive not simply from an unmediated set of holy texts, but *from his own experience* in a Christian community interacting, as he does himself, with the texts.

Hays' search for an ethical 'vision' embracing all New Testament writings opens up new vistas on Hebrews as an ethical work, even though he does not say a great deal about specific texts in Hebrews! It features nine times in his index (to 400 pages). He does claim, however, that if his three lenses are used, rather than that of *agape* love, Hebrews comes into clear focus as part of the moral vision of the New Testament (p 201). This idea of a vision which shapes the community illuminates Hebrews greatly. I would add that the predominant 'vision' of Hebrews, is the idea of 'looking unto Jesus,' as the way to maintain the community.

Hays' search for an ethical 'vision' embracing all NT writings opens up new vistas on Hebrews as an ethical work

Hays is not all about broad brush 'visions.' He rounds off his book with case-studies, citing Heb 10.32f in arguing that the NT rejects violence and retaliation but sees innocent suffering as a high virtue. He mentions 13.4 in his discussion of marriage and divorce, and in the background to discussion of homosexual behaviour.

But finally, I would disagree with Hays' assertion that 'freedom from law' is not a significant lens through which to study NT ethics. Hebrews sheds light on how his assertion should be modified. It says a great deal about Old Testament history and ritual as a shadow of things to come, which could not offer a deep enough remedy for the troubled conscience (9.11–14). The proposition should be rephrased as 'freedom from the mutual criticism or uneasy conscience which comes from fear of breaking the law.' If we do this, James and the Pastorals fall into line and possibly Matthew too (chapter 23?). The place of moral regulation in other books, even Paul's letters, becomes easier to square with a doctrine of salvation through grace.

Particular Issues in the Letter to the Hebrews 3

Hebrews raises some issues which may or may not have been in the writer's mind, at least as we now see them.

Some might now be classed as ecclesiastical rather than moral questions; for our author Christian life drew church, community and morality into a seamless robe. The church was a moral community as much as a religious, ethnic, or spiritual association.

Anti-Semitism

The roots of modern anti-Semitism have been seen in New Testament writings. Strictly this is an anachronism, since they are largely written about a Jew by Jews for Jews, and any critique of Jewish practice is an in-house dispute, like the disputes in the Dead Sea Scrolls. The danger came when Non-Jews, who were not part of their Jewish context, began treating these writings as their own, out of context. The cry of the crowd—'His blood be upon us…' (27.25)—or exchanges between 'Judaeans' and Jesus in John (for example 8.31–59) all too easily justified a Mediaeval pogrom.

The argument of Hebrews certainly centres around the continued relevance of Jewish institutions

The argument of Hebrews certainly centres around the continued relevance of Jewish institutions. It suggests a built-in obsolescence in those institutions such that they needed to be fulfilled through Jesus. It urges the readers not to drift back (2.1, 3) to the old institutions and the community which still observes them.

That old community may have felt threatened by this upstart group which followed a new and 'living' way, and had a record of inviting people to move across (though there is no hint of that in Hebrews). In a modern setting this kind of threat to an old established minority community (whether Jewish or Islamic) gives rise to accusations of racism. This dynamic would have been particularly acute if our writer's intention in urging his readers 'not to give up meeting…' (10.25), and to maintain 'brotherly love' (13.1) was to integrate his Jewish group with a wider Gentile church.

But remember, this letter dates from before the polarization of Judaism into the Rabbinic Judaism we now know, or even of Christianity as a distinct non-Judaism. Our writer sees the old covenant as a 'shadow of the good things to come' (10.1) but uses its Scriptures and handles them within Jewish parameters. He is still proud of that heritage, which prefigures what he now upholds and whose members can look forward to the fulfilment of their hopes in the new covenant community of which he writes (11.40). Though an invitation to 'go forth outside the camp…' (13.13) might be sensed in modern parlance to be 'anti-Semitic' by those 'inside,' that is hardly the author's intention. That, in Ellingworth's phrase (p 69), is 'not polemical but pastoral.' His vision is a fulfilled Judaism. For the record, our author uses quotations from the Song of Moses (Deut 32.35f//Heb 10.30) which Paul, and writers outside the NT (and the Qumran sect!), used polemically to criticize *Jewish* unbelief, to warn *his own Christian* readers.

Rigorism, and Apostasy

Our author intended to dissuade his readers from relapsing into the Judaism they had known before 'tasting the goodness of the word of God.' Much of his argument is theological, for the vision which they can grasp of Christ will shape their discipleship, but interwoven with that are pastoral exhortations, firm, but of loving intent. He is convinced that none of them has as yet gone as far as forgetting Christ's work (6.9), but he knows it is a present danger, for himself as much as for them (2.1, 3). The context is external hostility, but up to that point the readers' community had not shed blood for their faith. Compared with what was to follow from Nero to Diocletian their problems were minor. Encouragement is given in terms of mutual support, and loyalty to the church community; the language is of doctrine or fellowship. He does, however, talk about the impossibility of second repentance (6.4) and the absence of any sacrifice for 'wilful sin after receiving the knowledge of the truth' (10.26). Here the language is of wrong, though the context is of lapse, neglecting to keep fellowship and going back on commitment to Jesus. And for *these* readers relapse into Judaism (unlike a reversion to paganism) would not seem to be a lapse at all but merely a different way leading to the same one true God.

Of Hebrews 10.26 Bruce (p 258) comments that 'it was destined to have repercussions in Christian history beyond what our author could have foreseen.' As persecution became more intense the church faced the problem of those

He is convinced that none of them has as yet gone as far as forgetting Christ's work, but he knows it is a present danger

who had hidden or denied their faith yet wanted to renew it as pressure eased. Christians also recognized that they did continue to sin after their conversion and baptism, sometimes seriously. Was there a remedy, in the light of these passages? Or had our author overlooked or ignored this factor in human nature, despite what he says elsewhere about Christ's understanding and sympathy with it?

On one side Hermas (Rome, second century AD) revealed a one off, second repentance. Tertullian (North Africa, fl 200 AD) at first made provision for penitential discipline (in line with the church in Rome) but later (having turned Montanist—a rigorist sect) he denounced Hermas and the church in Rome for laxity in allowing second repentance. He understood 'wilful sin' in terms of sexual sin. Possibly in reaction to its apparent support of this Montanist rigorism, the second-century Roman presbyter Gaius rejected Pauline authorship (and so canonicity) of Hebrews (Ellingworth, p 38). The letter also influenced the later debates over betrayal in the face of imperial persecutions, while fear of post baptismal sin led some to defer baptism until their death-beds, notably the Emperor Constantine who perhaps anticipated a need for political sinning more than most.

So what can we say about our writer's intentions? He warns his readers about a particular danger, which they themselves have not hitherto seen as sinful. That danger is a relapse into their Jewish heritage. It amounts, he says, to adopting the view of those who crucified Jesus; it is a conscious rejection of him, since they should know better after having tasted how good he is. If Jesus' sacrifice is the only way to a truly clear conscience, to reject it is to move into a state in which the conscience cannot be cleared again. Bruce (p 118) notes how difficult it is, psychologically, for someone who has turned back from faith to accept it again. So is our author making an observation about psychology, rather than a statement of pastoral theology? Bruce does not claim so, and the writer talks about the non-availability of a further sacrifice, rather than the human possibilities of repentance.

Others look at the minutiae of what our writer says; he uses historic tenses to describe the original faith and then the lapse of these potential apostates, but then switches to present tenses to describe what their lapse amounts to (6.4ff). Should we then translate it: 'It is impossible to *go on renewing* again for repentance those who were enlightened...but did lapse (historic tenses), *so long as they continue to crucify* (present) *the Son of God...*'? This is a statement of the obvious; 'they can't repent until they repent'! The last phrase is explanatory; *'because they are crucifying...'* Having floated this idea Farrar (1894, p 84) prefers to cite the third century Montanists and Novatians, who denied the possibility not of divine forgiveness but of action by the church to reinstate the lapsed. In this case the odd phrase which I have rendered 'renew again for repentance' refers to baptism or similar action by the church. So is this a way of understanding our writer's intention? His concluding illustration, about an unfruitful crop, seems to go against it.

What our author does state is that he does not believe any of his readers have gone so far as to abandon their faith (6.9). His motive is to encourage people to hold on, not to denounce or exclude those who have fallen by the wayside. He was not intending to contribute to the Reformation disputes about the 'final perseverance of the saints' (or even third century discussions of betrayal) though by implication he would not (from the human side) bank on 'perseverance.'

In the same passage (6.9ff), too, he speaks of God's reliability and fair dealing towards those who honour him in their moral lives and Christian service. (6.10f). Though he was not writing in connection with 'final perseverance,' and though his strictures against apostasy serve to warn against a casual belief in the inevitability of salvation, he does point to the true basis for confidence in salvation—the faithfulness of God and a faith which has responded in practical Christian love.

The concern is not with detailed moral lapses so much as a failure to love the brethren enough to stick with them

In limited terms, then, he warned against a sin which could put people beyond repentance. He does not ask the church to exclude them.

As with the letters of John, the concern is not with detailed moral lapses so much as a failure to love the brethren enough to stick with them. The theological issues are different, and in Hebrews schism has not yet occurred, but in both cases it is separation from the fellowship which is *the* sin.

I nearly wrote at that point that such separation was 'unforgivable.' Perhaps that is what our author implied, but both Bruce (p 262) and Ellingworth (p 75f) point out that the author emphasizes the superior efficacy of Christ's forgiving sacrifice and his intercessory power such that what appears impossible—a new repentance and re-reception into the church through its normal means of reception—still, surely, remains within the power of God. Are they highlighting a contradiction in our author's logic, or themselves seeking to downplay the implications of a logic he understood and was at home with?

Conscience

Modern ethical thinking is used to the idea of conscience, not merely as retrospective reflection on conduct (so that we talk of a guilty or clear conscience), but also as a tool for planning future action (so that we talk of a conscientious decision), or as our character-based response to impromptu ethical dilemmas.

It is difficult to realize that such a concept, or at least the distinctive word to describe it, has not always been with us.

Background

The *experience* of 'conscience' is not a new thing, though changing social and religious norms colour the working of people's thought as they reflect on conduct. John Wilson (in Frankfort, pp 119–126) discusses the motives for social justice in ancient Egypt in terms of conscience, and cites an example (from the mid-second millennium BC) in which 'not sleeping at night' is a consideration. Dodds (pp 32–45, 55) traces the shift from a culture dominated by shame and honour in heroic Greece to one shaped by guilt that feared *pollution* (rather than *moral* guilt) in the golden age of Ancient Greece. Some writers were briefly conscious of weighing possible consequences and of anticipating regret at incurring this *'miasma.'* Their word is 'feeling a weight in the spirit' (*enthumion*) rather than self-consciousness (*syneidos*). Dodds discusses mythological images of 'conscience' — it is only a 'guilty conscience' that is in frame — but largely dismisses the idea; this is mechanistic fate, not inner moral turmoil.

Maurer, in his study of the New Testament words for conscience and self awareness, traces their development from classical Greek times. Euripides' Orestes describes his ailment; 'It is *synesis*, for I *know-in-myself* that I have done awful things.' But the 'awful things' relate to what infringes *taboo* — murder within the family — rather than general *moral guilt*, and are recognized by a rational, not subliminal process. Not until the second century BC does Polybius talk of *synesis* like a hostile witness, and the idea of a bad conscience gradually becomes common in secular Greek. But it means conscious reflection on past actions which are regretted. The idea of a 'good conscience' does not appear in non-Christian Greek until the mid-second century AD.

The Old Testament does not speak of a conscience as such. Maurer suggests that this is partly because God deals directly or through his law (Deut 30.14) with his people, though the word 'heart,' especially in the usage 'clean heart,' conveys the idea of a clear conscience. The Rabbis use similar language and see a good (or a bad) heart as the source of moral action. The Alexandrian Jewish writer Philo (first century AD) speaks of how (usually a bad) conscience tests out past action, but also sees this as a spur to good action or at least to conversion from bad practices; this testing can act as the conscience which prompts good action. (He does not use the word *syneidos* and its synonyms for this.) The idea perhaps comes from the Old Testament concept of examination in the sight of God (*ykch*) as much as from self awareness.

Overall, few parallels survive to the concepts of 'conscience' (here *syneidesis*) which develop in the New Testament, though Maurer does suggest that popular speech and local catch phrases (especially in Corinth) may have shaped the meaning. Its root denotes knowing oneself, without moral implications necessarily; Socrates is wise because he *knows his own* ignorance.

Hebrews

Hebrews does talk about Conscience in ways which are a distinct Christian development. It does not, however, represent the most extensive

Few parallels survive to the concepts of 'conscience' which develop in the New Testament

form of that development. The key change is that Christians can expect a *clear* conscience, free from the shadow of past wrongs or failings of which the self is conscious. This is best expressed in 1 Peter 3.21, with reference to baptism, which 'is an appeal to God for a good conscience, on the basis of the resurrection of Jesus Christ.' Christ's action on our behalf, laid hold of by baptism, makes the difference; the past is forgiven, its guilt—which is moral, not ritual—washed away.

Hebrews too sees baptism as the sign of latching on to the once for all time sacrifice of Christ the High Priest (10.22). It symbolizes forgiveness—the fact of the heart sprinkled clean from an evil conscience—a more effective purification than the repeated sacrifices of old Israel which left worshippers still conscious of sin (10.2). (The promise from Jeremiah 31.33f that God will write his laws on the minds of his new covenant people is quoted in this context, but not developed in relation to the 'forerunning' conscience shaping decisions in advance).

But our writer is clear that it is not the *ritual* of baptism, but the once for all sacrifice of Christ which purifies Christian believers and their conscience (9.9, 14). Here too the cleansing of the conscience frees up the believer to serve God—but the writer does not go so far as to say that the conscience is an active agent in shaping the nature of that service. 'Dead works' (given the way the pre-Christian world used *syneidesis*) probably refers to moral or ritual failings that play on the memory (perhaps in a life-sapping way) though they are dead and gone, not (as Protestants might wish) a lifeless reliance on moral probity or ritualism. The final use of Conscience in Hebrews (13.18) again has this positive sense; the writer (and his colleagues) have a clear (*kalos*, fine) conscience—it almost means 'quality of Christian life' as perhaps 1 Peter 3.16—so feels nothing can hinder his readers' prayers. Here the context does hint at how conscience may shape future conduct;

In Hebrews conscience is reflecting on motives rather than shaping actions

he wants to act well (*kalos*), but his conscience is reflecting on motives rather than shaping actions.

Fuller Developments

The fullest development of the idea of conscience is found in Paul's writings to the Corinthian and Roman churches. In discussing how to react to the dilemmas posed by meat from the market, possibly temple sacrifices, Paul considers how conscientious thinking about this will bear other people's consciences in mind as well as one's own. He has moved beyond the simple idea of a bad conscience to the idea that the conscience is the self-consciousness of the moral agent, which is aware not only of responsibilities to itself but also to others whose moral confidence is not so strong. In Corinthians it is not yet a distinct aspect of the personality, but is moving that way, and in 1 Cor 10.29 (RSV 'scruples') refers to a person's inner feelings about a course of action. In Romans (2.15) it is a characteristic in mankind (the verse refers to Gentiles) serving a parallel function to *Torah* among Jews, measuring their conduct and relationship to God. Significantly, though, when in Romans Paul discusses a similar issue to the one of sacrificial meat in 1 Corinthians, he uses the word 'faith' where in 1 Corinthians he used 'conscience.' This conscientious decision-making is sufficiently a core quality of the Christian life for it to be what faith works out as (see above re Heb 13.18, 1 Peter 3.16. Bultmann, 1, p 220, infers that *nous*, 'mind,' is similarly used to mean 'Christian ethical thinking' leading to moral action).

Maurer suggests that the use of *syneidesis* in Corinthians was due to a particular local catch-phrase. This may have been so, but Romans was written from Corinth so why is *syneidesis* not used in that letter too? I suspect that in Romans Paul wished to evoke particular reference to James, who had written of the value of 'unwavering faith' (though with different denotation, James 1.6, compare Rom 14.23 and 4.20). New Testament writers were struggling to find the right way of describing a developing concept. The clear conscience—the sense of freedom from guilt, and (in Paul) the consequent freedom to make moral decisions before God without incurring guilt—lay at the heart of the new Christian experience, so that for our writer it could be a characteristic description of the Christian lifestyle (Heb 13.20, compare 1 Peter 3.16). Ironically, his warnings against sin after sanctification led to anxiety over the possibility of forgiveness—an uneasy conscience!

Holiness

Our writer's characteristic description of Jesus is as the great high priest, so it is not surprising that 'sanctification' is his characteristic way of talking about entry into the Christian community (2.11, 10.10, 13.12), and holiness of life (12.10) is the purpose of our belonging to it. This reflects his vision of the fire of God's holiness. Holiness is something which is given to believers as a result of Jesus' sacrificial death, and also something which his readers should strive for by moral (but not ritual) conduct (12.14). Though he does not argue this explicitly his approach contrasts with that of his Rabbinic contemporaries. He was confident of the benefits won for us by a great high priest, rather than seeking to extend the standards of holiness expected from members of the priestly caste to the wider Jewish community. He links this holiness to peace with all people and avoidance of bitterness (with its knock-on effects on those around it) and immoral conduct (12.14ff—irreligion here is illustrated by Esau's casual regard for God's gifts).

He does not go into great detail about sins which might hinder holiness any more than the Johannine letters do. Like them he sees apostasy particularly as a sin, with the potential to exclude from the church and even from salvation itself. But this, by definition, is only a danger to those who have tasted the heavenly gift (6.4). As for where his readers have come from, twice he speaks of 'dead works' (6.1, 9.14) but this, like the word sin itself, is probably a general term. It covers any actions which played on the conscience.

This does not mean that our writer was unconcerned about conduct. He shares with the Johannine letters a vision for maintaining fellowship within the church and actually spells out in more detail what holy living entails. Chapter 13, integrated as it is with the rest of the letter (Filson, 1967, pp 13–26) details how this is worked out in a Christian congregation at its 'sectarian' stage —as a partly beleaguered group needing to maintain identity over against its root community and the wider world (see for example Wilson, p 36ff). The key word is *brotherly-love*, corresponding to John's 'love one another.' Our writer's vision of love includes a wider circle than John's. Strangers are to be shown hospitality. Though this may refer to travelling Christians, many commentators deem 'those in prison' and 'those who are ill-treated' (13.3) not to include just Christians. The motive is sympathy and fellow humanity. The implications of close fellowship might strain the marriage bond so its sanctity is reinforced—though this also reflects a challenge to laxity in wider society. The danger of greed is highlighted (elsewhere the readers' generosity is commended). In this there are parallels with Paul's letters to Timothy (mentioned at 13.23). Perhaps most significantly (Filson, p 80) our writer sees moral goodness as a sacrifice, replacing the physical sacrifices of the Jerusalem temple which no longer have relevance (13.15f and 12.28). Again he is expressing thoughts found in the Pauline corpus (Rom 12.1f) and parts of the Old Testament (for example Psalm 50.14). There are hints also in the Rabbis (m Abot 1.2 with 1.18, expressing a move over two centuries from temple service, law and kindness to truth, justice and peace).

To conclude, holiness is integrated with the letter's main message; the trials for which the writer prepares his readers are a discipline which will enable them to share God's holiness (12.10, 11).

Theodicy

In formal terms our author's answer to the great question of how God can allow suffering (at least the specific suffering facing his readers) is that it is part of a father's education of his children. Perhaps more than he knew, however, his letter, with its high Christology and vision of the suffering Christ, offers an emotional understanding which can reach deeper than an intellectual explanation. God in Christ has been here too. Here is 'sym–pathy'—true standing alongside.

'Neighbour-love'

On p 10 I refer to the use of 'neighbour' in modern liturgies and ethical discussion. Though it does not feature at all in Hebrews, it perhaps merits a detached comment! Similarly, because it forms part of that discussion, the word *agape*—the New Testament's characteristic word for 'Christian love'—deserves some comment, though I have given it fuller treatment in *The Ethics of the Johannine Epistles*, Grove Ethics booklet E 129 p 10f. As noted there, it denotes *practical* as much as emotional love. (*Pace* Sanders)

The Hebrew word *re$^{a'}$* meant someone living close by, but also had the connotation, similar to 'brother' ('a<u>h</u>) of someone belonging to the community of Israel. When Jesus was asked to explain and apply the commandment (Lev 19.18) 'you shall love your neighbour as yourself,' which in context applies to 'the sons of your own people,' he extended it, in the parable of the Good Samaritan, to include the outsider. From this parable, even though it is a single source (Luke 10.30ff), modern Christian ethicists such as Fletcher elevated 'Neighbour-love' to be *the* cardinal Christian principle, by which is meant a love which knows no social or ethnic bounds. (The writer to the Hebrews would probably have said 'No, it should be holiness.')

From this stems the rather idiosyncratic use of 'neighbour' in liturgies such as *Common Worship* (p 169) as a politically correct alternative to 'our fellow men' (as in ASB p 120). For those familiar with the parable this makes sense, but I wonder whether what we mean is clear to people who think of *Neighbours* as the inhabitants of a certain well-televised close in Australia! The liturgical denotation is almost the opposite to the popular connotations of the word!

4

'Looking unto Jesus'– A Slant on Imitatio Christi

I have suggested that Hebrews is a very ethical work, though not in a conventional modern sense.

It asks its readers to behave in particular moral ways, and remain within a particular moral community, and to encourage one another to resist sin (3.13). It chides them for not yet being teachers of right and wrong (5.14). Its final chapters offer specific examples of moral thinking and behaviour, interwoven with spirituality. For our writer, as for any serious Jew, spirituality cannot be divorced from behaviour. Far from following Sanders in seeing the 'Christian' element of the ethics in Hebrews 'awash,' and relegated to mere 'good citizenship,' we must affirm that here we have an ethic which lives and breathes its Christ-centred identity. Far from 'lacking motivation' the whole letter resonates with the thunder of motivation!

For our writer, as for any serious Jew spirituality cannot be divorced from behaviour

Christian Halakhah?

Recall the description of the primitive church in Acts (9.2) as followers of 'the Way.' John (14.6) reports Jesus saying 'I am the Way...' It comes as no surprise for our writer to speak of a 'new and living way' into God's presence through Jesus' sacrifice (10.19ff). We could understand this, and the John passage, in mystical ways, focusing just on our identification with Christ and our reliance on his self-offering. I suggest, however, that this plays down the force of the word 'way.' This is the *halakhah*, the way of life which Jesus both teaches and personifies. *Halakhah* is a Hebrew word meaning walk or *way*. It is the word which describes lifestyle teaching among the Rabbis (including for them ritual and cultural as well as ethical observance). While the Christian 'Way' was different from Rabbinic *halakhah*, I suggest it did connote lifestyle as well as devotion.

In chapter 13 we see some of the details of that lifestyle itemized—hospitality, sympathy, chastity, lack of greed, loyalty to past example (and in 12.15, a lack of bitterness and an irenic attitude in the face of assault). We are led on to a confidence in what Christ has achieved and so to an identification with him, within a worshipping community. (We should note that these points, which seem run of the mill morality for 19th and 20th century commentators, were not always so; some are classed as distinctly *spiritual* gifts' by Paul and Peter). The letter ends with prayer that God will graciously equip the readers to do his will, confirming that the writer's intention is to build the Christian lifestyle as well as the Christological perception of his readers. Theirs are the actions, but the inspiration is from God (13.20).

Before the itemized detail comes the grand picture. Chapter 12 paints this in terms of theodicy (in face of persecution) and gratitude, with warning examples. The readers' conflict is against *sin* (v 4) not just hostile authorities. (The writer does not go into detail about sin; presumably that was 'elementary, to be left behind,' 6.1). To lay aside the sin (from which Jesus has purified them, 12.1, compare 1.3) they should 'look to Jesus.' He endured hostility, and in earlier chapters the writer has pointed out that what he endured fitted him for what he did (2.10, 18). If 'one who is Son' endured this training, the readers too should see what they are going through as a paternal discipline. Unpleasant though it is, it is a sign of belonging (v 8) and will lead on to right living on the part of those who accept it (v 11). Their reaction to it should be conciliation, avoiding the bitterness which defiles both the inner life and relationship with God (vv 14, 15); they should be motivated by gratitude for their welcome into the unshakeable New Jerusalem and its cleansed community (vv 18–24, 28). Though God's awesome judgment is in the picture, the culmination of this sequence of motives is that they have come to Jesus, whose blood speaks forgiveness and grace. And if their *motivation* comes from a vision of Christ, *the purpose* of God's action and theirs is the attainment of holiness (vv 10, 14) and righteousness, avoiding immorality or profanity (vv 11, 16). The 'old' ethics of Murray catches the flavour of Hebrews better than some later 'trendy' versions.

The Imitation of Christ?

In chapter 12 our writer points his readers to Jesus as the trailblazer who brings their faith to fulfilment. In the bulk of the letter he has described how Jesus' work is more effective than the old covenant means of approach to God. One motive for remaining within the moral community is therefore that the alternatives are not effective, but there is another strand in our writer's moral vision. Christ is an example, *Our writer points his readers to Jesus as the trailblazer who brings their faith to fulfilment* but not just in the sense that here is someone to imitate. Our motive is not simply *'imitatio Christi,'* though that is part of the picture (12.3). He too 'endured.' It is almost as if *he has imitated us*, and so understands our situation, so that readers can draw inspiration and moral energy from that fact. Thus the Christological passages of 2.9–18 and 4.14f, 5.7–10 are an integral part of the moral encouragement of the letter. (Indeed, the whole of chaptes 1–10 fit this role. They explain how the readers receive the 'kingdom that cannot be shaken' (12.28) for which proper, worshipful, gratitude is shown in moral as well as devotional living). So, it is because Christ has been tested that he is able to help those who face their testing now (2.18, NEB).

'...not unable to sympathize...'

This vision of Christ the suffering supporter introduces a challenging moral dimension to Christology. Later Christological formulations avoided this, preferring to develop a static affirmation of Christ's divine and human natures (Greek philosophy was happier with discussing eternal realities than dynamic possibilities). Our writer certainly affirms the humanity and the divine son-ship of Jesus and indeed his perfection, and these thoughts contributed to the later discussion. In his view, however, that perfection was a dynamic process, not an eternal state. He is made perfect, or achieves the fulfilment of his life's work, through suffering (2.10). Perhaps the writer has Christ's death alone in mind here (compare 2.9) but the drift of the chapter is his likeness to his 'brethren' in *every* way. This is plainer in chapter 5, where we are told that 'although he was Son he learned obedience from what he suffered, and having been made perfect he became worthy of an eternal salvation for those who obey him...' (5.8ff). This perfection was not a once and for all time state, but the outcome of right responses to ongoing trying circumstances, leading at the end of the course to the fulfilment of his purpose. (This is a vision which matches well the developing picture in the gospels and Christ's responses there to injustice or attack).

Modelling Morality

Our writer does not develop perfection through suffering as a moral model for his readers. On one hand they are brought to glory or holiness through the transaction Christ has completed, *not* through their own suffering. They are to see suffering as *paideia* — discipline in the sense of education or upbringing, rather than punishment (12.7). They have 'become beneficiaries of Christ.' But on the other hand their part is to 'hold that state which they began with firm to the end' (3.14) and to strive for holiness of life and to be open to the grace of God.

They are to see suffering as discipline, in the sense of education or upbringing, rather than punishment

For the most part the moral models he does choose are people who are already Old Testament heroes. Such a pattern of teaching, based upon exemplary characters, is well known from contemporary Greek and Jewish writers. Ecclesiasticus 44–46 is a list of national(istic!) heroes; 1 Maccabees 2.52ff offers a similar list to demonstrate that none who put their trust in God shall be overcome (v 61). Philo also uses lists to encourage hope (*Rewards*, 11—archetypal craftsmen), and to argue that nobility is not merely inherited (*Virtues*, 198ff—the patriarchs and others).

In contrast our writer, realistically, gives examples not only of those who 'founded kingdoms' but also those who 'were sawn in two,' to encourage a faith which will look beyond human success stories to grasp the reality of what cannot be seen in earthly terms. And they are not simply moral examples. They are part of the team. Their 'perfection' depends on participation in what the readers now enjoy (11.40) and the force of their example is not least that they stuck fast to their allegiance without seeing in their own time the benefits of the great high priest.

Chapter 11 is the particular location of this character-building by exemplar. He cites personalities elsewhere who are often theological types, or foils to contrast with Jesus, rather than moral examples. However, Abraham's endurance (a key thought in the letter) is noted (6.15), while Esau is a negative model in 12.16. So, in passing, is the Exodus generation (3.16f). Heb 6.12 has a general encouragement to imitate 'those who' through faith and patience inherit God's promises, and 13.7 contains a similar encouragement with reference to former community leaders.

Grace or Effort?

I noted above what amounts to a tension, if not a contradiction, in our writer's thought. Christians are made what they are by Christ's unique self-offering, and this brings a freedom of conscience which transcends what has gone before. Nonetheless, they are to strive to obtain God's grace, and to avoid apostasy. So strong is the emphasis in the letter on not falling away (for example 6.4–8) that the author has been accused of reintroducing the idea of salvation by one's own effort (6.10, 10.36, see on Schrage, above), despite his affirmation of the once and for all efficacy of Jesus' offering (10.14).

Perhaps he had himself been taken aback by the prospect of his fellow Christians lapsing from their faith, so as to write so vehemently about the danger of such lapse. It seems that his view of Christ's work is that it is largely retrospective, cleansing the conscience from what has sullied it in the past, so that the forgiven believer is free to live right and keep the faith for the future (see Bultmann 2, p 168). His closing prayer (13.20f) probably sums up his feeling of how things ought to be; God will equip his people so that they can do his will, and he will work in them to bring this about. It is a co-operative venture between the forgiven believer and his Lord. His is the ethics of the clean slate, the fresh start relying on the wonder of acceptance, rather than regret and the goad of the guilty conscience. Faced with his readers' cooling ardour the writer's response is to warn them and urge them on more eloquently. He does not seem to consider more deeply the nature of ongoing repentance or a need for some penitential support (contrast Gal 6.1, James 5.16, 1 John 5.16 — but see below on Heb 6.3).

*God will equip his peopl
so that they can do his
will, and he will work i
them to bring this abou*

Like John in similar circumstances (1 John 2.1ª) he expects his readers not to sin. Unlike John he looks only at the big picture of apostasy, and says little about lesser sins or ongoing confession (compare 1 John 1.9, 5.16). Christ's intercession is seen to relate to the believers' initial appeal to him (Heb 7.25) rather than to continued forgiving advocacy (1 John 2.1ᵇ). For him the tension is not the Reformation contrast between 'grace' and 'works,' but the puzzle of how to react when grace does not appear to be working. 'How are we to escape if we neglect so great a salvation?' (Heb 2.3). Because it is the big issue of apostasy which is in view for him, his response is to say 'Persevere, it is worth it, there is no alternative.' (As for the lesser issues, has he perhaps consciously decided that this is not the time or place to deal with them? 'This we will do if God permits' [6.3 — if that is a fair understanding of this verse]). But even as he says 'Try harder' he is offering his readers not a theory of prevenient grace but practical advice on how to let God's grace work — by mutual encouragement, and by developing the gratitude which comes from the enlarged vision which he paints of all Christ has done for them.

*He is offering his
readers not a theory of
prevenient grace but
practical advice on how
to let God's grace work*

Conclusions

5

Hebrews is a letter with a very large moral vision. Its majestic view of Christ offers a motive for readers' conduct, whether in the first or twenty-first century. This is what he has done for us; this is how he understands us; this is how he expects us to build holy lives.

This lifestyle is learned within a sanctified community, in which mutual encouragement and practical support work alongside our corporate vision of Christ and our hope of an eternal home. This challenges modern, individualistic (and secular) approaches to morality. It still offers a model for teaching and learning Christ-centred living today, in churches which may be dulled by apathy rather than threatened with persecution, and tempted to drift, with little sense of discrimination, into a generalized religion.

> *So let us lay aside the sin which hampers us, and run the race before us, focusing on Jesus, our trailblazer and final escort in faith.*

Select Bibliography

F F Bruce, *The Epistle to the Hebrews* (London: (NICNT), 1965)

R Bultmann, *Theology of the New Testament 1* (tr K Grobel) (London: SCM Press, 1952, [2]1965)

R Bultmann, *Theology of the New Testament 2* (tr K Grobel) (London: SCM Press, 1955, [2]1965)

H Danby (tr), *The Mishnah* (Cambridge: CUP, 1933)

E R Dodds, *The Greeks and the Irrational* (Berkley, University of California Press, 1951)

P Ellingworth, *The Epistle to the Hebrews* (Carlisle: Paternoster, 1993)

F W Farrar, *The Epistle of Paul the Apostle to the Hebrews* (Cambridge, 1894)

F V Filson, *Yesterday* (London: SCM Press, 1967)

H Frankfort, *et al, Before Philosophy* (Harmondsworth: Pelican, 1949)

D Guthrie, *Hebrews* (Leicester: Tyndale NTC, 1993, 1983)

R B Hays, *The Moral Vision of the New Testament* (Edinburgh: T&T Clarke, 1996)

J L Houlden, *Ethics and the New Testament* (Edinburgh: T&T Clarke, ²1992, originally Oxford: Mowbray's, 1975)

G Kittel (and G Friedrichs), *Theological Dictionary of the New Testament VII* (Grand Rapids, Michigan: Eerdmans, 1971)

Maurer, in Kittel and Freidrichs, TDNT vii, p 898ff, *Synoida*...

H Montefiore, *A Commentary on the Epistle to the Hebrews* (London: A&C Black, 1964)

J Murray, *Principles of Conduct* (London: Tyndale Press, 1957)

J A T Robinson, *Redating the New Testament* (London: SCM Press, 1976)

J T Sanders, *Ethics in the New Testament* (London: SCM Press, 1975)

W Schrage, *The Ethics of the New Testament* (tr D E Green) (Edinburgh: T&T Clarke, 1988)

C Spicq, *Epitre aux Hebreux* (Paris: Libraire Le Coffre, 1952)

B Wilson, *Religious Sects* (London: Weidenfeld & Nicholson, 1970)

Tom Wright, *Hebrews for Everyone* (London: SPCK, 2003)

C D Yonge (trans), D M Scholer (ed), *The Works of Philo* (Hendrickson, 1993)